tourism TATTLER
Issue 03 March 2016

PUBLISHER
Tourism Tattler (Pty) Ltd.
PO Box 891, Umhlanga Rocks, 4320
KwaZulu-Natal, South Africa.
Website: *www.tourismtattler.com*

EXECUTIVE EDITOR Des Langkilde
Cell: +27 (0)82 374 7260
Fax: +27 (0)86 651 8080
E-mail: *editor@tourismtattler.com*
Skype: tourismtattler

MAGAZINE ADVERTISING
ADVERTISING DIRECTOR Bev Langkilde
Cell: +27 (0)71 224 9971
Fax: +27 (0)86 656 3860
E-mail: *bev@tourismtattler.com*
Skype: bevtourismtattler

SUBSCRIPTIONS
http://eepurl.com/bocIdD

BACK ISSUES (Click on the covers below).

Contents

05 BUSINESS: Wikitourism.

11 ENVIRONMENT: The Global Impact of Environmental Tourism.

30 EVENTS: Big Ideas for Green Meetings.

IN THIS ISSUE

EDITORIAL
04 Accreditation

BUSINESS
05 Wikitourism
06 SATSA Market Intelligence Report
07 SA Budget Speech & Tourism Sector
08 Travel Trade Challenges in 2016 Part 2

COMPETITION
10 Win a set of wildlife DVDs

ENVIRONMENT
11 Impact of Environmental Tourism

EVENTS
17 Big Ideas for Green Meetings

HOSPITALITY
18 Kenya's weird and wonderful hotels
20 Part-time Hotel Qualifications
22 TripAdvisor at 16, The Facts

LEGAL
23 The Consumer Protection Act - Part 2

RISK
24 Tourism Insurance - Part 3

TRANSPORT
26 Overland Tour Vehicle of Choice

TRADE NEWS
Visit our website for daily news updates

EDITORIAL CONTRIBUTORS
Adv. Louis Nel
Adrienne Harris
Christa Badenhorst
Des Langkilde
Dr. Peter E. Tarlow
Jessica Ndlovu
Kagiso Mosue
Martin Janse van Vuuren
Peter Corcoran

MAGAZINE SPONSORS
02 Fancourt
19 Spier Wine Farm
21 Gooderson Monks Cowl
28 National Sea Rescue Institute

Disclaimer: The Tourism Tattler is published by Tourism Tattler (Pty) Ltd and is the official trade journal of the Southern Africa Tourism Services Association (SATSA). The Tourism Tattler digital e-zine, is distributed free of charge to bona fide tourism stakeholders. Letters to the Editor are assumed intended for publication in whole or part and may therefore be used for such purpose. The information provided and opinions expressed in this publication are provided in good faith and do not necessarily represent the opinions of Tourism Tattler (Pty) Ltd, SATSA, its staff and its production suppliers. Advice provided herein should not be soley relied upon as each set of circumstances may differ. Professional advice should be sought in each instance. Neither Tourism Tattler (Pty) Ltd, SATSA, its staff and its production suppliers can be held legally liable in any way for damages of any kind whatsoever arising directly or indirectly from any facts or information provided or omitted in these pages or from any statements made or withheld or from supplied photographs or graphic images reproduced by the publication.

Add Fancourt to your Conference Bucket List

ONLY 7KM FROM GEORGE AIRPORT, WITH DAILY FLIGHTS FROM MAJOR CITIES, DELEGATES CAN CHOOSE FROM 115 FANCOURT HOTEL ROOMS AND 18 MANOR HOUSE SUITES AND AN ASSORTMENT OF LEISURE ACTIVITIES – GIVING BUSINESS TRAVELLERS MORE THAN SIMPLY CONFERENCING AND BANQUETING.

MEETINGS, INCENTIVES, CONFERENCES & EVENTS

- Fully equipped conference centre, meeting and events venue
- Large multi-purpose ballroom on the upper floor
- Six meeting rooms situated on the upper levels
- Spacious foyers on two levels
- Capacity from small groups to 400
- All meeting rooms have natural daylight
- On-site technician and IT support

WINTER AT FANCOURT – THE PERFECT TIME

- Underfloor heating and heated towel rails
- Warm scented and personalised towels
- Luxury hot chocolate and marshmallow turndowns
- Heated indoor pool, gym and instruction studio
- Heated therapeutic Roman Bath and Luxury Spa
- Wood-fired pizza venue with complimentary Glühwein
- No rumbling tummies with our 5 star hot breakfast buffet!

Terms and conditions apply
Group Reservations 044 804 0020 or groupreservations@fancourt.co.za
www.fancourt.com

BOOKING CODE: 16GCWTT

BOKAY DESIGNS

078 894 1811 • info@bokaydesigns.co.za • www.bokaydesigns.co.za

As a freelance designer I strive to combine simplicity with technical functionality in digital, social and print communications.

WEBSITE DESIGN
I leverage the powerful WordPress publishing platform to build awesome, mobile responsive websites that rank well and are easy for clients to manage.

GRAPHIC DESIGN
I develop creative ideas and concepts, choosing the appropriate media and style to meet my client's objectives. Projects are undertaken from start to finished product.

SOCIAL MEDIA
I can help you with set-up and/or daily monitoring and posts for your business to grow your social influence and generate sales leads.

Save **10% off** your first project!   078 894 1811

Accreditation

Official Travel Trade Journal and Media Partner to:

The Africa Travel Association (ATA)
Tel: +1 212 447 1357 • Email: info@africatravelassociation.org • Website: www.africatravelassociation.org

ATA is a division of the Corporate Council on Africa (CCA), and a registered non-profit trade association in the USA, with headquarters in Washington, DC and chapters around the world. ATA is dedicated to promoting travel and tourism to Africa and strengthening intra-Africa partnerships. Established in 1975, ATA provides services to both the public and private sectors of the industry.

The African Travel & Tourism Association (Atta)
Tel: +44 20 7937 4408 • Email: info@atta.travel • Website: www.atta.travel

Members in 22 African countries and 37 worldwide use Atta to: Network and collaborate with peers in African tourism; Grow their online presence with a branded profile; Ask and answer specialist questions and give advice; and Attend key industry events.

National Accommodation Association of South Africa (NAA-SA)
Tel: +2786 186 2272 • Fax: +2786 225 9858 • Website: www.naa-sa.co.za

The NAA-SA is a network of mainly smaller accommodation providers around South Africa – from B&Bs in country towns offering comfortable personal service to luxurious boutique city lodges with those extra special touches – you're sure to find a suitable place, and at the same time feel confident that your stay at an NAA-SA member's establishment will meet your requirements.

Regional Tourism Organisation of Southern Africa (RETOSA)
Tel: +2711 315 2420/1 • Fax: +2711 315 2422 • Website: www.retosa.co.za

RETOSA is a Southern African Development Community (SADC) institution responsible for tourism growth and development. RETOSA's aims are to increase tourist arrivals to the region through. RETOSA Member States are Angola, Botswana, DR Congo, Lesotho, Madagascar, Malawi, Mauritius, Mozambique, Namibia, Seychelles, South Africa, Swaziland, Tanzania, Zambia and Zimbabwe.

Southern Africa Tourism Services Association (SATSA)
Tel: +2786 127 2872 • Fax: +2711 886 755 • Website: www.satsa.com

SATSA is a credibility accreditation body representing the private sector of the inbound tourism industry. SATSA members are Bonded thus providing a financial guarantee against advance deposits held in the event of the involuntary liquidation. SATSA represents: Transport providers, Tour Operators, DMC's, Accommodation Suppliers, Tour Brokers, Adventure Tourism Providers, Business Tourism Providers and Allied Tourism Services providers.

Southern African Vehicle Rental and Leasing Association (SAVRALA)
Contact: manager@savrala.co.za • Website: w

Founded in the 1970's, SAVRALA is the representative voice of Southern Africa's vehicle rental, leasing and fleet management sector. Our members have a combined national footprint with more than 600 branches countrywide. SAVRALA are instrumental in steering industry standards and continuously strive to protect both their members' interests, and those of the public, and are therefore widely respected within corporate and government sectors.

Seychelles Hospitality & Tourism Association (SHTA)
Tel: +248 432 5560 • Fax: +248 422 5718 • Website: www.shta.sc

The Seychelles Hospitality and Tourism Association was created in 2002 when the Seychelles Hotel Association merged with the Seychelles Hotel and Guesthouse Association. SHTA's primary focus is to unite all Seychelles tourism industry stakeholders under one association in order to be better prepared to defend the interest of the industry and its sustainability as the pillar of the country's economy.

International Coalition of Tourism Partners (ICTP)
Website: www.tourismpartners.org

ICTP is a travel and tourism coalition of global destinations committed to Quality Services and Green Growth.

International Institute for Peace through Tourism
Website: www.iipt.org

IIPT is dedicated to fostering tourism initiatives that contribute to international understanding and cooperation.

World Travel Market
WTM Africa - Cape Town in April, WTM Latin America - São Paulo in April, and WTM - London in November. WTM is the place to do business.

World Youth Student and Educational (WYSE) Travel Confederation
Website: www.wysetc.org

WYSE is a global not-for-profit membership organisation.

The Safari Awards
Website: www.safariawards.com

Safari Award finalists are amongst the top 3% in Africa and the winners are unquestionably the best.

World Luxury Hotel Awards
Website: www.luxuryhotelawards.com

World Luxury Hotel Awards is an international company that provides award recognition to the best hotels from all over the world.

BUSINESS & FINANCE

Wiki Tourism

Access to tourism-related information has become a lot easier with South Africa's home-grown Wikitourism online portal. All content is publicly available with copyright permission, which means that anyone can freely use the information, writes **Adrienne Harris**.

Anyone with access to a computer these days will know about Wikipedia - and has probably even quoted from it numerous times.

But there's a new Wiki on the block – Wikitourism, the information portal for the tourism industry, by the tourism industry. This project has been initiated by the Tourism Enterprise Partnership (TEP), which has long had 'access to information' as a key pillar of providing support to small tourism businesses in South Africa. The challenge has always been how this can best be achieved.

Tourism industry information has been uploaded onto numerous websites, which makes it extremely difficult to source information - in fact, a quick Google search on the words 'tourism industry information South Africa' came up with just over 99 million results. A further difficulty with doing general searches is that many (if not most) of these 99 million webpages do not exist anymore, or have been moved, or are simply out of date. Keeping websites up to date takes up substantial resources, and many man-hours. It is also important that the user of any web-based information is confident in the accuracy of the information accessed.

TEP, as the word 'partnership' in its name shows, has always looked to collaboration as means to maximise resources for truly effective impact. And Wikitourism is no different. Taking on the ethos of creative commons used by Wikipedia and various open source initiatives, Wikitourism has been developed as a free information portal for the benefit of the entire tourism industry. All articles, documents and other information are either publicly available, have copyright permission or have been written specifically for the website. This means that anyone can freely use this information.

As with the concept of Wikipedia, Wikitourism relies on dedicated tourism role-players who are prepared to contribute their time and knowledge to build up a repository of information of use to all types of tourism stakeholders. The initial incubation of the project has been undertaken by TEP, but as Dr Salifou Siddo, the TEP Chief Executive, explained, "we are hoping that industry individuals and associations will start to 'own' sections of the website and ensure that these sections are kept up to date and relevant. This includes trade associations, academics, specialists and anyone else who feels that they have information to contribute".

There is no doubt that there is a huge demand for information – the current statistics from Wikitourism bear this out. The site now boasts

www.wikitourism.com

more than 154 000 unique page visits and nearly 600 000 page reads. These statistics not only show that Wikitourism is now firmly embedded as a source, but also that visitors are not just looking at the home page and quitting out. The ratio of page reads to unique visits shows that users are not just looking at the home page and quitting out.

TEP is encouraging all role-players in the industry to get involved. Whilst 'Wiki-ing' as a contributor takes a bit of getting used to, the software has been designed to allow for quick uploads, edits and additions. In fact, the word 'Wiki' comes from the Hawaiian word 'quick' and this website is certainly growing "Wiki, wiki". This is another great advantage of using MediaWiki software as opposed to more traditional web-based software, the website can grow with great ease. The amount of information that can be added is virtually limitless, although it is unlikely that Wikitourism will ever compete in size with Wikipedia's 39 million pages!

Wikitourism is an absolute game-changer when it comes to how we handle "information overload" in the tourism industry, and it is all thanks to committed individuals who are prepared to support and promote access to information for all stakeholders.

About the author: Adrienne Harris is the Executive Director of Harvest Tourism - a company that focusses on tourism development as a tool for poverty alleviation, community benefication, training, strategic planning and implementation. For more information email adrienneh@tep.co.za or visit www.wikitourism.co.za

BUSINESS & FINANCE

SATSA Market Intelligence Report
Southern Africa Tourism Services Association BONDED*
Grant Thornton

The information below was extracted from data available as at **03 March 2016**. By **Martin Jansen van Vuuren** of **Grant Thornton**.

ARRIVALS

The latest available data from **Statistics South Africa** is for **January to December 2015***:

	Current period	Change over same period last year
UK	407 486	1.4%
Germany	256 646	-6.5%
USA	297 226	-3.9%
India	78 385	-8.5%
China (incl Hong Kong)	84 878	2.2%
Overseas Arrivals	2 144 988	-4.9%
African Arrivals	6 746 114	-7.3%
Total Foreign Arrivals	8 903 773	-6.8%

HOTEL STATS

The latest available data from **STR Global** is for **January to December 2015**:

Current period	Average Room Occupancy (ARO)	Average Room Rate (ARR)	Revenue Per Available Room (RevPAR)
All Hotels in SA	63.4%	R 1 086	R 688
All 5-star hotels in SA	63.0%	R 1 981	R 1 249
All 4-star hotels in SA	62.6%	R 1 024	R 641
All 3-star hotels in SA	63.4%	R 871	R 552
Change over same period last year			
All Hotels in SA	1.4%	6.5%	8.0%
All 5-star hotels in SA	1.3%	9.5%	11.0%
All 4-star hotels in SA	2.2%	5.3%	7.6%
All 3-star hotels in SA	-0.2%	6.2%	5.9%

ACSA DATA

The latest available data from **ACSA** is for **January** 2016:

Change over same period last year	Passengers arriving on International Flights	Passengers arriving on Regional Flights	Passengers arriving on Domestic Flights
OR Tambo International	5.1%	8.4%	14.9%
Cape Town International	-0.1%	39.5%	16.7%
King Shaka International	6.6%	N/A	15.7%

CAR RENTAL DATA

The latest available data from **SAVRALA** is for **January to June 2015**:

	Current period	Change over same period last year
Industry rental days	8 139 127	-1%
Industry utilisation	70.2%	-0.7%
Industry Average daily revenue	2 498 944 728	1%

WHAT THIS MEANS FOR MY BUSINESS

Analyses of Statistics South Africa data shows that foreign arrivals declined in 2015 and were at similar levels to 2013. A ray of hope is that foreign arrivals did start to increase in the last quarter of 2015. As stated in previous report, the tourism industry in South Africa is currently being propped up by domestic tourism as evident in the increase in arrivals on domestic flights. It is hoped that the depreciation of the Rand coupled to the implementation of the revised visa regulations will lead to a full recovery in the growth of foreign arrivals to supplement domestic tourism. *Note that African Arrivals plus Overseas Arrivals do not add to Total Foreign Arrivals due to the exclusion of unspecified arrivals, which could not be allocated to either African or Overseas. As from January 2014, Stats SA stopped counting people transiting through SA as tourists. As a result of the revision, in order to compare the 2015 figures with 2014, it has been necessary to deduct the transit figures from the 2014 totals.

For more information contact Martin at Grant Thornton on +27 (0)21 417 8838 or visit: http://www.gt.co.za

South Africa Budget Speech Acknowledges Travel & Tourism Sector

BUSINESS & FINANCE

The 2016 budget speech has demonstrated that Government is beginning to fully appreciate the meaningful role that the travel and tourism sector plays in the South African economy, writes **Kagiso Mosue**.

In his 2016 budget speech delivered on Wednesday 24 February, the Minister of Finance, Hon. Pravin Gordhan made mention of measures taken to strengthen the travel and tourism sector and the overall recognition of its economic contribution. The Tourism Business Council of South Africa ("TBCSA") is pleased to note the Minister's comments regarding Government's initiative to provide policy certainty and to 'address institutional and regulatory barriers to business investment and growth'. Travel and tourism is one of the key areas wherein the country has a definite competitive advantage and the TBCSA believes that collaboration is critical to ensure that the country ultimately reaps the benefits that many countries have reaped by supporting their travel and tourism sector.

Against the backdrop of low economic growth, high unemployment and drought, TBCSA acknowledges the tough juggling act that the Minister has had to achieve in order to deliver a 'balanced' budget which goes some way to respond to these and many other challenges the country is facing.

Proposals on various elements highlighted in the speech present a number of challenges as well as opportunities for the travel and tourism sector:

Investment and Sustainable Growth

With the increased funding allocation for the Industrial Development Corporation (IDC), the Council looks forward to the IDC expanding its involvement in the travel and tourism sector, not only in the hospitality sphere, but also other segments which require also infrastructural investment such as business tourism. In addition, the New Development Bank, presents another avenue for businesses in the sector – particularly those with interests in other parts of regional Africa – to source funding for further investment.

Going forward, TBCSA plans to align itself with other organised business formations, to urge Government to do more to inject some positive energy in the economy, which will further stimulate private sector investment

Fiscal Consolidation

TBCSA recognises the urgent need for Government to curtail expenditure, amid a slowdown in revenue and a growing budget deficit. However, it remains concerned about the potential negative implications that expenditure cuts in Government procurement of travel, accommodation and conferencing services are likely to have on the sector. The Council wishes for an opportunity to engage with Treasury on the proposed national travel and accommodation policy and instructions on conference costs to ensure minimal negative impact on trade.

Tax Proposals

With rising inflation, we are all likely to feel the effects of the proposed tax proposals. However, from a sector perspective, hospitality and tourism transport (particularly small businesses) are likely to be the hardest hit by the increases in the fuel levy, the introduction of a sugar tax and tyre levy amongst other taxes which are already in place. Despite these inflationary pressures, the TBCSA hopes the tax relief in personal income will go some way in putting some money back in the pocket of the travel consumer.

State-Owned Entities

In the Minister's own words, State-Owned Entities have important roles to play in boosting growth and development. It is with this in mind that the travel and tourism private sector welcomes plans to create a more operationally efficient airline. As a national carrier, TBCSA believes that SAA should play a more significant role and be a major partner to our sector in driving travel and tourism locally, regionally and internationally.

As highlighted in the speech, much work needs to be done to contain public sector spending and to improve the efficiencies at many of the SOEs. In this regard, the travel and tourism is anxiously hoping that through NERSA, the Government will review the increment requested by Eskom for electricity in the country as it will add to the woes that are already cumbersome to business and the public.

Overall, TBCSA is encouraged by the Minister Gordhan's budget speech, particularly the inclusion of travel and tourism in Government's action plans going forward. As a sector that touches every facet of the economy, this renewed focus on the sector is set to go a long way in helping the country to achieve its economic imperatives of creating jobs and creating a viable environment for business to thrive.

About the author: Ms. Kagiso Mosue is the Corporate Communications Manager at the Tourism Business Council of South Africa (TBCSA) – a member-based organisation made up of Tourism Associations as well as leading businesses operating in the Travel and Tourism sector. TBCSA seeks to ensure that the industry is unified and speaks with one voice when engaging relevant stakeholders on macro-economic issues affecting the sector. For more information visit www.tbcsa.travel

BUSINESS & FINANCE

Travel Trade Challenges in 2016
- PART 2 -

Last month we examined some of the challenges facing the tourism industry in 2016. This month we examine related challenges with which tourism leaders may have to contend in 2016, writes **Dr. Peter E. Tarlow**.

It should be noted that although the material in both the February and March editions is treated as separate challenges, there is often an interaction between them, and these challenges are not stand alones but rather part of a total whole.

Be prepared for economic instability

We are now seeing the stock market on a roller coaster and coupled with low gas prices, there is a sense of ennui and foreboding. Last year's feel good combination has now changed to one of wait-and-see in the United States, Latin America and Europe.

Experts indicate that there are multiple clouds on the horizon. These include an unstable European economy, recession in countries such as Brazil and low employment rates, and a slowing down of the Chinese economy. It is essential to remember that although unemployment is low in the US, this figure does not necessarily reflect a strong economy, but rather that millions of people have ceased looking for work. In this world of false recoveries, low unemployment does not translate into the willingness on the part of the public to travel more.

View the world carefully

The political world will continue to be unstable and when instability hits, people are less likely to spend money on luxury items such as travel. Political instability is now a major concern in Africa and Latin America, with the Middle East, Europe, and North America open to terrorism attacks and Latin America still suffering from high levels of crime and drug trafficking. Furthermore, no one knows how Europe's refugee crisis will play out and what the consequences of increased crime will be on European tourism. Brazil, along with much of Latin America, is suffering from both issues of crime and issues of health and sanitation.

Be aware of the lack of trained personnel

Because many tourism areas have grown rapidly there are too many locations where there is a dearth of skilled labor. Tourism needs people who are both inspired and well trained. Yet, too few people in the tourism industry speak multiple languages, are proficient in high tech computer skills or have a good knowledge of statistics and how to utilize them. This lack of education and training creates not only numerous financial losses but also creates lost opportunities and an inability to adapt to new challenges.

Low Salaries, recruitment and retention

Many online and front-line workers receive low salaries, have low levels of job loyalty, and change jobs with a high level of rapidity. This high turnover level makes training difficult and often each time a person leaves, the information is lost. To make matters even more challenging these are often the people with whom visitors come into contact. The formula tends to guarantee low job satisfaction and low levels of customer satisfaction. This situation has resulted in the lack of availability of skilled manpower in the travel and tourism industry, one of the largest, if not the largest, employment generators in the world. If tourism is to be a sustainable product then it needs to turn part-time jobs into careers without pricing itself out of the market. If the travel and tourism industry hopes to continue to grow it will need trained personnel, and a willing and enthusiastic workforce at every level from managerial, to skilled workers, to semi-skilled workers.

Nonsensical regulations and over regulation

No one is arguing that tourism should be an unregulated industry, but often governments' desire to regulate trumps common sense. All too often decisions are made so as to avoid a law suite or negative media coverage. Too many regulations are reactive to problems that are minimal, while refusing to be proactive regarding growing problems. Often the desire to over-regulate puts tourism businesses in jeopardy and fails to help the consumer.

Lack of adequate and truthful marketing

Too many locations tend to either exaggerate or simply fabricate. The lack of truth in marketing means that the public not only loses confidence in the industry but investors fear being burnt. Marketing has to be both innovative and true. Tourism is a highly competitive industry and requires good and innovative marketing that captures a place's essence while making people aware of the locale's tourism offerings.

Lack of amenities or over charging for amenity use

In too many locations around the world there is a lack of simple amenities. From clean and potable water at hotels to well maintained public rest rooms. Finding simple public services in these locations is a constant challenge. Signage is often unintelligible to foreign tourists,

BUSINESS & FINANCE

parking turns an outing into a nightmare, and as hard as it seems to believe there are all too many 'good quality' hotels that charge for internet service. In many locations the hotel's in-room phone service is outrageously expensive even for local calls. The lack of amenities or over charging for their usage destroys the sense of hospitality and turns guests into mere customers.

Need to develop or update tourism infrastructure

Around the world tourism suffers from poor infrastructure. These infrastructure challenges range from substandard docks and ports of entry to modes of transport, to urban infrastructure such as access roads, electricity, water supply, sewerage and telecommunication. As airplanes begin to carry more people, airports will face not only the problems of handling large numbers of arriving passengers but will also need to find ways to unload luggage faster, and transit people through immigration and customs lines more rapidly. The lack of infrastructure will also impact issues of security as governments attempt to ferret out potential terrorists while creating a warm and welcoming arrival experience.

Airline industry will continue to be the part of tourism that visitors love to hate

Air travel has gone from elegant to pedestrian. Today passengers are crowded onto planes as if they were cattle, and treated as if they were criminals rather than honored guests. Airfares are so complicated that passengers need a college course to understand them, and the once popular airline loyalty programs continue to degenerate. Service is often so bad that when flight attendants smile, passengers actually thank them. Unfortunately the "getting there" has become part of the "being there", and unless the tourism industry can work with the airline industry to change attitudes, be less mercenary and more flexible the entire industry may suffer. When poor air service is combined with infrastructure problems the combination may in the long run be deadly and "staycations" may over take vacations.

Nothing works if visitors are afraid and insecure.

The spread of terrorist groups throughout the world, and what seems to be the *"pandemic du jour"* are major threats to tourism. Tourism must learn to create not merely security and safety but 'surety': the interaction between the two. This means that locations without TOPPs (tourism policing programs) will suffer and eventually decline. Private security and public security will need to learn to interact and work well not only with each other but with the media and marketers as well. The old and outdated adage that security scares visitors is more and more being replaced with the adage that the lack of security provokes fear among visitors. Cyber crime will continue to be another major challenge the travel industry faces. Tourism cannot merely hobble from pandemics and health crisis to the next. Also, unless the travel and tourism industry can protect visitor privacy and lower the incidents of fraud, it will face an ever greater and daunting challenge during 2016.

About the Author: Dr. Peter E. Tarlow publishes a monthly 'Tourism Tidbits' newsletter. He is a founder of the Texas chapter of TTRA, President of T&M, and a popular author and speaker on tourism. Tarlow is a specialist in the areas of sociology of tourism, economic development, tourism safety and security. Tarlow speaks at governors' and state conferences on tourism and conducts seminars throughout the world. For more information e-mail ptarlow@tourismandmore.com

Tourism Safety Initiative Gains Momentum

The Tourism Safety Initiative ("TSI") is rapidly gaining momentum as the South African travel and tourism industry's primary platform for the coordination, promotion and provision of safety support to tourists.

TSI is a travel and tourism private sector safety support initiative, managed and driven by the Tourism Business Council of South Africa (TBCSA). The Council recently appointed a dedicated project manager for TSI, Mr. Ian Janse van Vuuren, who has a long history of working within the intelligence and security environments. Furthermore, the TSI now boasts a simpler, newly-revamped online incident reporting portal.

The initiative operates on two legs:

1. Proactive risk management, which involves encouraging tourism businesses to report criminal incidents against tourists through the TSI portal. Based on inter alia these incident reports, the TSI will produce weekly, bi-weekly, monthly and quarterly research reports for select client groupings in this space. Incident reporting is encouraged, even in situations where the case has been opened with the South African Police Services.

2. Reactive incident management, which will see TSI in collaboration with other partners, offer emergency support to the affected businesses or individual tourists.

Whilst the proactive risk management aspect of the project is already active, work is currently underway to finalise finer details of a TSI reactive incident management system which will see the industry tap into a central resource for access to emergency tourist support where required.

TBCSA Chief Executive Officer, Ms. Mmatšatši Ramawela said TSI was an important project for the industry and that she was pleased with the renewed energy with which the project is being pursued. "A lot of work still lies ahead for us, but overall we are pleased with the progress that has been achieved thus far". She highlighted the alignment of TSI to regional and provincial tourism safety initiatives, the finalisation of the TSI emergency support model, agreement on messaging and the conclusion of Private-Public-Partnerships with relevant role-players as some of the major goals the initiative still has to reach.

On the issue of collaboration, Janse van Vuuren, echoed Ramawela's view, saying: "By our own admission we cannot do this by ourselves with the limited resources at our disposal". He underlined the importance of better collaboration within the industry, as well as with the authorities in order to address the issue of crimes targeted at tourists. "Remember, crime is the core business of criminals, but fighting crime is not the core business of the travel and tourism industry. This is fundamental paradox that will continue to favour criminals and their modus operandi until Private-Public Partnerships allows a better flow of information sharing and collaboration".

All incidents can be logged on the TSI website portal at: www.tourismsafety.co.za or sent via email to: info@tourismsafety.co.za

Competition

The winning 'Like' or 'Share' during the month of **March 2016** will receive a **two wildlife documentary DVD's: Patterns in the Grass and The Last Lion by Derek and Beverly Joubert** with the compliments of **Livingstones Supply Co – Suppliers of the Finest Products to the Hospitality Industry**.

'Like' / 'Share' / 'Connect' with these Social Media icons to win!

Livingston Supply Company

Tourism Tattler

Competition Rules: Only one winner will be selected each month on a random selection draw basis. The prize winner will be notified via social media. The prize will be delivered by the sponsor to the winners postal address within South Africa. Should the winner reside outside of South Africa, delivery charges may be applicable. The prize may not be exchanged for cash.

Congratulations to our February Social Media winner

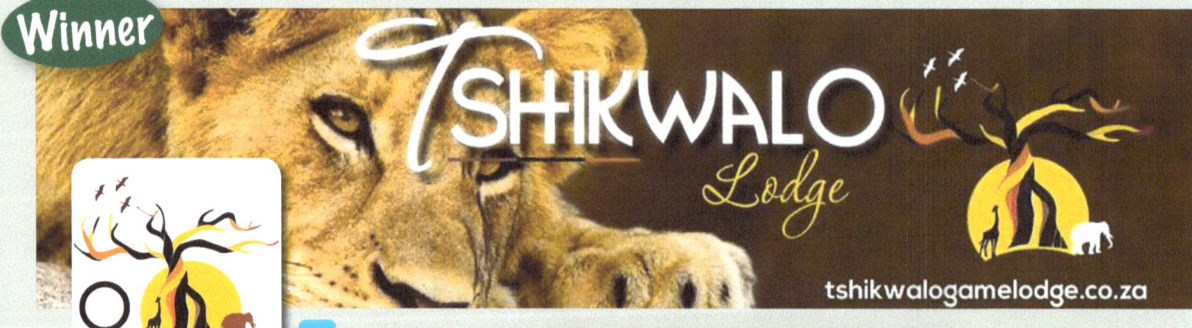

@tshikwalo

Tshikwalo Game Lodge in Dinokeng Game Reserve has been selected as our **February 2016** winner for their 'Follow & Tweet' on **Twitter**.
Tshikwalo will receive a **set of 5 Stonecast crockery pots** with the compliments of **Livingstones Supply Co – Suppliers of the Finest Products to the Hospitality Industry**.

For more information visit www.livingstonessupplyco.com

ENVIRONMENT

The Global Impact of Environmental Tourism

This informative article deals with the main impact areas of Environmental Tourism from a global perspective, and the environmental conservation aspect of Environmental Tourism.

Published with acknowledgement to the United Nations Environment Programme.

Environmental Tourism, which is also referred to as Ecotourism, Sustainable Tourism and Responsible Tourism, are terms rooted in the concept of development that "meets the needs of the present without compromising the ability of future generations to meet their own needs" *(Bruntland Commission, 1987)*.

Environmental Impacts

The quality of the environment, both natural and man-made, is essential to tourism. However, tourism's relationship with the environment is complex. It involves many activities that can have adverse environmental effects. Many of these impacts are linked with the construction of general infrastructure such as roads and airports, and of tourism facilities, including resorts, hotels, restaurants, shops, golf courses and marinas. The negative impacts of tourism development can gradually destroy the environmental resources on which it depends.

On the other hand, tourism has the potential to create beneficial effects on the environment by contributing to environmental protection and conservation. It is a way to raise awareness of environmental values and it can serve as a tool to finance protection of natural areas and increase their economic importance.

Tourism's Three Main Impact Areas

Negative impacts from tourism occur when the level of visitor use is greater than the environment's ability to cope with this use within the acceptable limits of change. Uncontrolled conventional tourism poses potential threats to many natural areas around the world. It can put enormous pressure on an area and lead to impacts such as soil erosion, increased pollution, discharges into the sea, natural habitat loss, increased pressure on endangered species and heightened vulnerability to forest fires. It often puts a strain on water resources, and it can force local populations to compete for the use of critical resources.

1. Depletion of Natural Resources

Tourism development can put pressure on natural resources when it increases consumption in areas where resources are already scarce.

1a) Water resources

Water, and especially fresh water, is one of the most critical natural resources. The tourism industry generally overuses water resources for hotels, swimming pools, golf courses and personal use of water by tourists. This can result in water shortages and degradation of water supplies, as well as generating a greater volume of waste water.

In drier regions like the Mediterranean, the issue of water scarcity is of particular concern. Because of the hot climate and the tendency of tourists to consume more water when on holiday than they do at home, the amount used can run up to 440 liters a day. This is almost double what the inhabitants of an average Spanish city use.

Golf course maintenance can also deplete fresh water resources. In recent years golf tourism has increased in popularity and the number of golf courses has grown rapidly. Golf courses require an enormous amount of water every day and, as with other causes of excessive extraction of water, this can result in water scarcity. If the water comes from wells, overpumping can cause saline intrusion into groundwater. Golf resorts are more and more often situated in or near protected areas or areas where resources are limited, exacerbating their impacts.

An average golf course in a tropical country such as Thailand needs 1500kg of chemical fertilizers, pesticides and herbicides per year and uses as much water as 60,000 rural villagers. (Source: Tourism Concern).

1b) Local resources

Tourism can create great pressure on local resources like energy, food, and other raw materials that may already be in short supply. Greater extraction and transport of these resources exacerbates the physical impacts associated with their exploitation. Because of the seasonal character of the industry, many destinations have ten times more inhabitants in the high season than in the low season. A high demand is placed upon these resources to meet the high expectations tourists often have (proper heating, hot water, etc.).

The Global Impact of Environmental Tourism (Cont'd)

1c) Land degradation

Important land resources include minerals, fossil fuels, fertile soil, forests, wetland and wildlife. Increased construction of tourism and recreational facilities has increased the pressure on these resources and on scenic landscapes. Direct impact on natural resources, both renewable and nonrenewable, in the provision of tourist facilities can be caused by the use of land for accommodation and other infrastructure provision, and the use of building materials.

Forests often suffer negative impacts of tourism in the form of deforestation caused by fuel wood collection and land clearing. For example, one trekking tourist in Nepal - and area already suffering the effects of deforestation - can use four to five kilogrammes of wood a day.

2. Pollution

Tourism can cause the same forms of pollution as any other industry: air emissions, noise, solid waste and littering, releases of sewage, oil and chemicals, even architectural/visual pollution.

2a) Air pollution and noise

Transport by air, road, and rail is continuously increasing in response to the rising number of tourists and their greater mobility. To give an indication, the International Civil Aviation Organisation (ICAO) reported that the number of international air passengers worldwide rose from 88 million in 1972 to 344 million in 1994. One consequence of this increase in air transport is that tourism now accounts for more than 60% of air travel and is therefore responsible for an important share of air emissions. One study estimated that a single transatlantic return flight emits almost half the CO_2 emissions produced by all other sources (lighting, heating, car use, etc.) consumed by an average person yearly. (*Mayer Hillman, Town & Country Planning magazine, September 1996. Source: MFOE*).

Transport emissions and emissions from energy production and use are linked to acid rain, global warming and photochemical pollution. Air pollution from tourist transportation has impacts on the global level, especially from carbon dioxide (CO_2) emissions related to transportation energy use. And it can contribute to severe local air pollution. Some of these impacts are quite specific to tourist activities. For example, especially in very hot or cold countries, tour buses often leave their motors running for hours while the tourists go out for an excursion because they want to return to a comfortably air-conditioned bus.

Noise pollution from airplanes, cars, and buses, as well as recreational vehicles such as snowmobiles and jet skis, is an ever-growing problem of modern life. In addition to causing annoyance, stress, and even hearing loss for it humans, it causes distress to wildlife, especially in sensitive areas. For instance, noise generated by snowmobiles can cause animals to alter their natural activity patterns.

2b) Solid waste and littering

In areas with high concentrations of tourist activities and appealing natural attractions, waste disposal is a serious problem and improper disposal can be a major despoiler of the natural environment - rivers, scenic areas, and roadsides. For example, cruise ships in the Caribbean are estimated to produce more than 70,000 tons of waste each year. Today some cruise lines are actively working to reduce waste-related impacts (Refer: Cruise Lines International Association). Solid waste and littering can degrade the physical appearance of the water and shoreline and cause the death of marine animals.

In mountain areas, trekking tourists generate a great deal of waste. Tourists on expedition leave behind their garbage, oxygen cylinders and even camping equipment. Such practices degrade the environment with all the detritus typical of the developed world, in remote areas that have few garbage collection or disposal facilities. Some trails in the Peruvian Andes and in Nepal frequently visited by tourists have been nicknamed "Coca-Cola trail" and "Toilet paper trail".

2c) Sewage

Construction of hotels, recreation and other facilities often leads to increased sewage pollution. Wastewater has polluted seas and lakes surrounding tourist attractions, damaging the flora and fauna. Sewage runoff causes serious damage to coral reefs because it stimulates the growth of algae, which cover the filter-feeding corals, hindering their ability to survive. Changes in salinity and siltation can have wide-ranging impacts on coastal environments. And sewage pollution can threaten the health of humans and animals.

2d) Aesthetic Pollution

Often tourism fails to integrate its structures with the natural features and indigenous architectural of the destination. Large, dominating resorts of disparate design can look out of place in any natural environment and may clash with the indigenous structural design.

A lack of land-use planning and building regulations in many destinations has facilitated sprawling developments along coastlines, valleys and scenic routes. The sprawl includes tourism facilities themselves and supporting infrastructure such as roads, employee housing, parking, service areas, and waste disposal.

3. Physical Impacts

Attractive landscape sites, such as sandy beaches, lakes, riversides, and mountain tops and slopes, are often transitional zones, characterized by species-rich ecosystems. Typical physical impacts include the degradation of such ecosystems.

An ecosystem is a geographic area including all the living organisms (people, plants, animals, and microorganisms), their physical surroundings (such as soil, water, and air), and the natural cycles that sustain them. The ecosystems most threatened with degradation are ecologically fragile areas such as alpine regions, rain forests, wetlands, mangroves, coral reefs and sea grass beds. The threats to, and pressures on, these ecosystems are often severe because such places are very attractive to both tourists and developers.

In industrial countries, mass tourism and recreation are now fast overtaking the extractive industries as the largest threat to mountain communities and environments. Since 1945, visits to

the 10 most popular mountainous national parks in the United States have increased twelve-fold. In the European Alps, tourism now exceeds 100 million visitor-days. Every year in the Indian Himalayas, more than 250,000 Hindu pilgrims, 25,000 trekkers, and 75 mountaineering expeditions climb to the sacred source of the Ganges River, the Gangotri Glacier. They deplete local forests for firewood, trample riparian vegetation, and strew litter. Even worse, this tourism frequently induces poorly planned, land-intensive development. Source: People & the Planet.

Physical impacts are caused not only by tourism-related land clearing and construction, but by continuing tourist activities and long-term changes in local economies and ecologies.

3a) Physical impacts of tourism development

3ai) Construction activities and infrastructure development. The development of tourism facilities such as accommodation, water supplies, restaurants and recreation facilities can involve sand mining, beach and sand dune erosion, soil erosion and extensive paving. In addition, road and airport construction can lead to land degradation and loss of wildlife habitats and deterioration of scenery.

In Yosemite National Park (US), for instance, the number of roads and facilities have been increased to keep pace with the growing visitor numbers and to supply amenities, infrastructure and parking lots for all these tourists. These actions have caused habitat loss in the park and are accompanied by various forms of pollution including air pollution from automobile emissions; the Sierra Club has reported "smog so thick that Yosemite Valley could not be seen from airplanes". (Source: Trade and Environment Database)

3aii) Deforestation and intensified or unsustainable use of land. Construction of ski resort accommodation and facilities frequently requires clearing forested land. Coastal wetlands are often drained and filled due to lack of more suitable sites for construction of tourism facilities and infrastructure. These activities can cause severe disturbance and erosion of the local ecosystem, even destruction in the long term.

3aiii) Marina development. Development of marinas and breakwaters can cause changes in currents and coastlines. Furthermore, extraction of building materials such as sand affects coral reefs, mangroves, and hinterland forests, leading to erosion and destruction of habitats. In the Philippines and the Maldives, dynamiting and mining of coral for resort building materials has damaged fragile coral reefs and depleted the fisheries that sustain local people and attract tourists.

Overbuilding and extensive paving of shorelines can result in destruction of habitats and disruption of land-sea connections. Coral reefs are especially fragile marine ecosystems and are suffering worldwide from reef-based tourism developments.

Evidence suggests a variety of impacts to coral result from shoreline development, increased sediments in the water, trampling by tourists and divers, ship groundings, pollution from sewage, overfishing, and fishing with poisons and explosives that destroy coral habitat.

3b) Physical impacts from tourist activities

3bi) Trampling: Tourists using the same trail over and over again trample the vegetation and soil, eventually causing damage that can lead to loss of biodiversity and other impacts. Such damage can be even more extensive when visitors frequently stray off established trails.

3bii) Anchoring and other marine activities. In marine areas (around coastal waters, reefs, beach and shoreline, offshore waters, uplands and lagoons) many tourist activities occur in or around fragile ecosystems. Anchoring, snorkeling, sport fishing and scuba diving, yachting, and cruising are some of the activities that can cause direct degradation of marine ecosystems such as coral reefs, and subsequent impacts on coastal protection and fisheries.

3biii) Alteration of ecosystems by tourist activities. Habitat can be degraded by tourism leisure activities. For example, wildlife viewing can bring about stress for the animals and alter their natural behavior when tourists come too close. Safaris and wildlife watching activities have a degrading effect on habitat as they often are accompanied by the noise and commotion created by tourists as they chase wild animals in their trucks and aircraft. This puts high pressure on animal habits and behaviors and tends to bring about behavioral changes. In some cases, as in Kenya, it has led to animals becoming so disturbed that at times they neglect their young or fail to mate.

There are 109 countries with coral reefs. In 90 of them reefs are being damaged by cruise ship anchors and sewage, by tourists breaking off chunks of coral, and by commercial harvesting for sale to tourists. One study of a cruise ship anchor dropped in a coral reef for one day found an area about half the size of a football field completely destroyed, and half again as much covered by rubble that died later. It was estimated that coral recovery would take fifty years. (Source: Ocean Planet).

The Wider Caribbean Region, stretching from Florida to French Guiana, receives 63,000 port calls from ships each year, and they generate 82,000 tons of garbage. About 77% of all ship waste comes from cruise vessels. The average cruise ship carries 600 crew-members and 1,400 passengers. On average, passengers on a cruise ship each account for 3.5 kilograms of garbage daily - compared with the 0.8 kilograms each generated by the less well-endowed folk on shore. (Source: Our Planet).

The Global Impact of Environmental Tourism (Cont'd)

Environmental Impacts of Tourism

Loss of Biological Diversity

Biological diversity is the term given to the variety of life on Earth and the natural patterns it forms.

The effects of loss of biodiversity:

- It threatens our food supplies, opportunities for recreation and tourism, and sources of wood, medicines and energy.
- It interferes with essential ecological functions such as species balance, soil formation, and greenhouse gas absorption.
- It reduces the productivity of ecosystems, thereby shrinking nature's basket of goods and services, from which we constantly draw.
- It destabilises ecosystems and weakens their ability to deal with natural disasters such as floods, droughts, and hurricanes, and with human-caused stresses, such as pollution and climate change.

Tourism, especially nature tourism, is closely linked to biodiversity and the attractions created by a rich and varied environment. It can also cause loss of biodiversity when land and resources are strained by excessive use, and when impacts on vegetation, wildlife, mountain, marine and coastal environments and water resources exceed the carrying capacity. This loss of biodiversity in fact means loss of tourism potential.

Introduction of exotic species

Tourists and suppliers - often unwittingly - can bring in species (insects, wild and cultivated plants and diseases) that are not native to the local environment and that can cause enormous disruption and even destruction of ecosystems.

Depletion of the Ozone Layer

The ozone layer, which is situated in the upper atmosphere (or stratosphere) at an altitude of 12-50 kilometres, protects life on earth by absorbing the harmful wavelengths of the sun's ultraviolet (UV) radiation, which in high doses is dangerous to humans and animals. For instance, one of the reasons scientists have put forward for the global decrease of amphibian populations is increased exposure to UV radiation.

Ozone depleting substances (ODSs) such as CFCs (chlorofluorocarbon) and halons have contributed to the destruction of this layer. The tourism industry may be part of the problem; direct impacts start with the construction of new developments and continue during daily management and operations. Refrigerators, air conditioners and propellants in aerosol spray cans, amongst others, contain ODSs and are widely used in the hotel and tourism industry. Emissions from jet aircraft are also a significant source of ODSs. According to *Tourism Concern*, scientists predict that by 2015 half of the annual destruction of the ozone layer hd been caused by air travel. UNEP's OzonAction Programme works with governments and industries, including the tourism industry, to phase out ODSs and find safer alternatives. UNEP has developed extensive information and guidance on how many types of businesses can eliminate ODSs and contribute to preservation of the ozone layer. For further reading see the publication How the Hotel and Tourism Industry can Protect the Ozone Layer.

Climate Change

Climate scientists now generally agree that the Earth's surface temperatures have risen steadily in recent years because of an increase in the so-called greenhouse gases in the atmosphere, which trap heat from the sun. One of the most significant of these gases is carbon dioxide (CO_2), which is generated when fossil fuels, such as coal, oil and natural gas are burned (e.g. in industry, electricity generation, and automobiles) and when there are changes in land use, such as deforestation. In the long run, the accumulation of CO_2 and other greenhouse gases in the atmosphere can cause global climate change - a process that may already be occurring.

Global tourism is closely linked to climate change. Tourism involves the movement of people from their homes to other destinations and accounts for about 50% of traffic movements; rapidly expanding air traffic contributes about 2.5% of the production of CO_2. Tourism is thus a significant contributor to the increasing concentrations of greenhouse gases in the atmosphere. (Source: Mountain Forum)

Air travel itself is a major contributor to the greenhouse effect. Passenger jets are the fastest growing source of greenhouse gas emissions. The number of international travellers is expected to increase from 594 million in 1996 to 1.6 billion by 2020, adding greatly to the problem unless steps are taken to reduce emissions. (Source: WWF)

For more information on the relationship between energy and the environment, see UNEP's Energy Programme, which provides information and publications on energy efficiency and alternative energy sources to reduce the environmental impacts of energy use and of transportation.

How Environmental Impacts affect Tourism

Natural disasters. Catastrophes like floods, earthquakes, wildfires, volcanoes, avalanches, drought and diseases can have a serious effect on inbound and domestic tourism and thus on local tourism industries. The outbreak of the foot and mouth disease epidemic in England earlier this year (2001), for instance, has severely affected Great Britain's inbound tourism market. A BHA/Barclays Hospitality Business Trends Survey found that 75% of hotels in England, 81% in Scotland and 85% in Wales continued to be affected by the foot and mouth outbreak, and over 60% forecast a decline in business in the June-September 2001 period.

Climate Change. Tourism not only contributes to climate change, but is affected by it as well. Climate change is likely to increase the severity and frequency of storms and severe weather events, which can have disastrous effects on tourism in the affected regions. Some of the other impacts that the world risks as a result of global warming are drought, diseases and heat waves.

These negative impacts can keep tourists away from the holiday destinations. Global warming may cause:

- Less snowfall at ski resorts, meaning a shorter skiing seasons in the Alpine region. In already hot areas like Asia and the Mediterranean, tourists will stay away because of immense heat, and out of fear of diseases and water shortages.
- Harm to vulnerable ecosystems such as rainforests and coral reefs because of rising temperatures and less rainfall. A major risk to coral reefs is bleaching, which occurs when coral is stressed by temperature increases, high or low levels of salinity, lower water quality, and an increase in suspended sediments. These conditions cause the *zooxanthallae* (the single-celled algae which forms the colours within the coral) to leave the coral. Without the algae, the coral appears white, or "bleached" - and rapidly dies. The Great Barrier Reef, which supports a US$ 640 million tourism industry, has been experiencing coral bleaching events for the last 20 years. (Source: EXN)
- Rising sea levels, the result of melting glaciers and polar ice. Higher sea levels will threaten coastal and marine areas with widespread floods in low-lying countries and island states, increasing the loss of coastal land. Beaches and islands that are major tourism attractions may be the first areas to be affected.
- Increased events of extreme weather, such as tornadoes, hurricanes and typhoons. These are already becoming more prevalent in tourist areas in the Caribbean and South East Asia. Hurricane Mitch in 1998, for instance, heavily affected tourism in the Caribbean. Wind damage, storm waves, heavy rains and flooding caused major losses in the local tourism sector.

Tourism and Environmental Conservation

The tourism industry can contribute to conservation through:

Direct financial contributions. Tourism can contribute directly to the conservation of sensitive areas and habitat. Revenue from park-entrance fees and similar sources can be allocated specifically to pay for the protection and management of environmentally sensitive areas. Special fees for park operations or conservation activities can be collected from tourists or tour operators.

The tour operator Discovery Initiatives, which is a member of the Tour Operators Initiative for Sustainable Tourism Development, makes an annual financial contribution to the Orangutan Foundation of some US$ 45,000. The money is earned from only 5 tour groups of 10 people each visiting the Tanjing Putting National Park in Central Kalimantan. The park is under huge pressures from deforestation and river pollution from unrestricted gold mining. This money directly funds park staff and rangers, rehabilitation efforts for young orangutans, and the care center. It provides almost the only economic support for saving this park, where the park fees are officially only the equivalent of 12 pence a day.

Contributions to government revenues. Some governments collect money in more far-reaching and indirect ways that are not linked to specific parks or conservation areas. User fees, income taxes, taxes on sales or rental of recreation equipment, and license fees for activities such as hunting and fishing can provide governments with the funds needed to manage natural resources. Such funds can be used for overall conservation programs and activities, such as park ranger salaries and park maintenance.

For Costa Rica, tourism represents 72% of national monetary reserves, generates 140,000 jobs and produces 8.4% of the gross domestic product. The country has 25% of its territory classified under some category of conservation management. In 1999, protected areas welcomed 866,083 national and foreign tourists, who generated about US$ 2.5 million in admission fees and payment of services.

Improved environmental management and planning. Sound environmental management of tourism facilities and especially hotels can increase the benefits to natural areas. But this requires careful planning for controlled development, based on analysis of the environmental resources of the area. Planning helps to make choices between conflicting uses, or to find ways to make them compatible. By planning early for tourism development, damaging and expensive mistakes can be prevented, avoiding the gradual deterioration of environmental assets significant to tourism.

Cleaner production techniques can be important tools for planning and operating tourism facilities in a way that minimizes their environmental impacts. For example, green building (using energy-efficient and non-polluting construction materials, sewage systems and energy sources) is an increasingly important way for the tourism industry to decrease its impact on the environment. And because waste treatment and disposal are often major, long-term environmental problems in the tourism industry, pollution prevention is especially important for the tourism industry.

Environmental awareness raising. Tourism has the potential to increase public appreciation of the environment and to spread awareness of environmental problems when it brings people into closer contact with nature and the environment. This confrontation may heighten awareness of the value of nature and lead to environmentally conscious behavior and activities to preserve the environment.

Protection and preservation. Tourism can significantly contribute to environmental protection, conservation and restoration of biological diversity and sustainable use of natural resources. Because of their attractiveness, pristine natural areas are valuable and the need to keep the attraction alive can lead to creation of national parks and wildlife parks.

Tourism has had a positive effect on wildlife preservation and protection efforts, notably in Africa but also in South America, Asia, Australia, and the South Pacific. Numerous animal and plant species have already become extinct or may become extinct soon. Many countries have therefore established wildlife reserves and enacted strict laws protecting the animals that draw nature-loving tourists. As a result of these measures, several endangered species have begun to thrive again.

ENVIRONMENT

The Global Impact of Environmental Tourism (Cont'd)

In the Great Lakes region of Africa, mountain gorillas, one of the world's most endangered great apes, play a critical ecological, economic and political role. Their habitat lies on the borders of northwestern Rwanda, eastern Democratic Republic of Congo and southwestern Uganda. Despite 10 years of political crisis and civil war in the region, the need for revenue from ape-related tourism has led all sides in the conflict to cooperate in protecting the apes and their habitat.

Establishment of a gorilla tracking permit, which costs US$ 250 plus park fees, means that just three habituated gorilla groups of about 38 individuals in total can generate over US$ 3 million in revenue per year, making each individual worth nearly US$ 90,000 a year to Uganda. Tourism funds have contributed to development at the local, national and regional level. The presence of such a valuable tourism revenue source in the fragile afromontane forests ensures that these critical habitats are protected, thus fulfilling their valuable ecological function including local climate regulation, water catchment, and natural resources for local communities. Source: UNEP Great Apes Survival Project and Discovery Initiatives.

Alternative employment. Tourism can provide an alternative to development scenarios that may have greater environmental impacts. The Eco-escuela de Español, a Spanish language school created in 1996 as part of a Conservation International project in the Guatemalan village of San Andres, is an example. The community-owned school, located in the Maya Biosphere Reserve, combines individual language courses with home stay opportunities and community-led eco-tours. It receives around 1,800 tourists yearly, mostly from the US and Europe, and employs almost 100 residents, of whom around 60% were previously engaged in mostly illegal timber extraction, hunting and milpas, or slash-and-burn agriculture. Careful monitoring in 2000 has shown that, among the families benefiting from the business, the majority has significantly reduced hunting practices, and the number and extension of "slash-and-burn" agricultural plots. Furthermore, as most families in the village benefit directly or indirectly from the school, community-managed private reserves have been established, and social pressure against hunting has increased.

Regulatory measures. Regulatory measures help offset negative impacts; for instance, controls on the number of tourist activities and movement of visitors within protected areas can limit impacts on the ecosystem and help maintain the integrity and vitality of the site. Such limits can also reduce the negative impacts on resources.

Limits should be established after an in-depth analysis of the maximum sustainable visitor capacity. This strategy is being used in the Galapagos Islands, where the number of ships allowed to cruise this remote archipelago is limited, and only designated islands can be visited,

Baby Mountain Gorilla in Virunga National Park © Cai Tjeenk Willink / Wikimedia Commons / Attribution-Share Alike 3.0 Unported.

About the United Nations Environment Programme (UNEP) Tourism and Environment Programme. Aware of and concerned about the negative environmental and social impacts of tourism, as well as the opportunities it offers, Ministers of the Environment have decided to give due consideration to this major issue with the aim of creating the adequate policy context to make the tourism industry sustainable. To that end, UNEP has been appointed by the Commission on Sustainable Development (CSD) as the Interagency Coordinator or lead agency responsible for implementation of Agenda 21 issues on tourism. Together with the World Tourism Organization, UNEP is the main focal point on sustainable tourism for CSD and the Convention on Biological Diversity.

For more information visit www.unep.org

EVENTS

4 Big Ideas 4 Green Meetings

The colour green is often associated with plants and nature, which is why the term 'green meetings' is associated with sustainable procurement practices.

Likewise, the idiom 'give the green light' means "go", so if you are working on a meeting or conference project and your boss gives you the 'green light', it means that he/she gives approval for the project to proceed.

With this in mind, here are 4 great ideas for green meetings and conferences that will 'give the green light' and make your peers 'green with envy':

1. Reduce paper

Business meetings and industry conferences use an enormous amount of paper in the form of writing pads, programmes, business cards and event sponsor brochures. Here are a few alternatives to replace these items with:

1a. Business Cards

Poken is a USB device that replaces printed business cards. Attendees simply touch their Poken devices together to transfer their contact details, and when back in the office simply plug the Poken into the computer USB port, log into the event portal (perviously emailed by the event organiser) to see all the people he/she has connected with. Documents can be downloaded, and business cards synchronised to Outlook, SalesForce, etcetera.

1b. Note taking

If you have to supply pens and writing pads, make sure that they are environment-friendly. For example, Spier provides recycled pens and paper, which meeting organisers can then donate to Spier's school programme after the event. Alternately, encourage attendees to make notes on their laptop, tablet or smartphone devices. Also upoad speaker presentations onto your event website.

2. Avoid plastic

Stop supplying plastic water bottles to quench the thirst of your meeting attenddes. Many hotel conference venues do provide glass water bottles. For example, Spier not only provide glass bottles but also fill them with purified water sourced from the farms own filtration system. Spier also recycles 100% of its wastewater. If possible, hand-write attendee names onto recycled board and if inserting them into plastic sleeve holders, make sure that these are collected after the meeting for reuse at the next event. Beaded lanyards are a good idea as these are usually hand crafted and support local communities. Spier uses Sue Heathcock Projects to source craft products.

3. Offset carbon emissions

Look for ways to reduce and neutralize the carbon emissions from attendees' flights – by far the biggest polluter. Perhaps donate an indigenous tree for each attendee to plant, or donate solar panels to a local community. Try to minimise the need for road transport by choosing venues and hotels that are close together, and encourage delegates to ride-share and use public transport. Also choose transport suppliers who use emissions-reduction technologies and can certify that their service is carbon-neutral.

4. Choose a green venue

Select a venue that has the following measures in place:
- An automated electricity-savings programme to prevent waste by lights, air conditioning and escalators;
- A water-use minimisation system that incorporates things like drip-flow irrigation and dual-flush toilets;
- An in-house recycling system;
- A food re-distribution programme;
- Use biodegradable cleaning agents; and
- Have a policy to source local supplies that promote job creation and the sustainability of local farms and producers.

Spier Wine Farm in Stellenbosch, South Africa ticks all of these boxes and more.

For a more comprehensive green guide download the 'Conscious Conferencing at Spier' interactive PDF or contact the Spier conference team on +27 (0) 809 1100 Ext 1 or email conference@spier.co.za

HOSPITALITY

Kenya's weird and wonderful hotels

Kenya has a wide range of weird and wonderful hotels – making the whole experience of travelling to Kenya, that much more exiting, writes **Jessica Ndlovu**.

When people think of travelling to Kenya, they think of scenic sights and wildlife not found anywhere else in the world. Kenya offers a range of stunning accommodation options, including family based hotels, luxurious lodges and also something a little bit different. Take the opportunity to experience some of the more unusual options, whether it involves eating breakfast alongside giraffes or settling in for the night in the high treetops overlooking the coast. Here are some of Kenya's most exciting but unusual stays:

Hippo Point, Nakuru

A hidden gem quite literally camouflaged amongst the natural landscape. Hippo Point is a quiet spot, home to over 350 species of birds and 1,200 resident animals. The eight-storey tower is so well camouflaged that the wildlife mistake it for a yellow acacia tree. Styled similarly to a pagoda, the top of the tower has a 360 degree observation tower and a meditation room, while on the ground floor you can walk alongside the zebras and giraffes which roam freely.

For more information visit www.hippopointkenya.com

Watamu Treehouse, Watamu

The Watamu Treehouse is one of the most unusual yet picturesque hotels on the Kenyan coast. Overlooking the Indian Ocean on one side and the forest on the other, there is no such thing as a bad view at the treehouse. In addition, there are no windows – only natural spaces where one can experience nature without any artificial barrier. Created by local artist and conservationist Nani Croze, the property uses local wood and strategic architectural design techniques to ensure guests are able to appreciate their surroundings in a serene and natural environment.

For more information visit www.treehouse.co.ke

Giraffe Manor, Nairobi

Giraffe Manor is a one-of-a-kind guesthouse where the resident Rothschild giraffes peek in to say hello every morning and quite literally, eat by your side over breakfast! Kenya is every wildlife lover's dream and Giraffe Manor offers the ultimate experience as guests can wake up in the luxurious rooms, and are welcomed by giraffes of all shapes and sizes which you can even reach out to and feed. Dating back to the 1930s, the charming manor can be found in the leafy areas of the country's capital, Nairobi.

For more information visit www.thesafaricollection.com

The Ark

Modelled after the biblical Noah's Ark, this hotel is just as attractive to animals and wildlife as the original. Due to its nearby waterhole and salt lick, the accommodation is a flytrap for Kenya's wildlife. Guests have the opportunity to spot wildlife from any of the four viewing decks. Never miss a trick as the staff press a buzzer to alert guests about animals of special interest visiting the waterhole.

For more information visit www.thearkkenya.com/

Loisaba Conservancy

Nestled within the beautiful stretches of land in Laikipia, the Loosaba Conservancy offers a night like no other – under the stars. Conveniently named 'Star Beds', the handcrafted wooden four-posters come complete with insect netting and overlook either the Kibakoko waterhole in the Eastern valleys or the Ewaso N'giro River.

For more information visit www.loisaba.com

About the author: *Jessica Ndlovu as a PR intern for* Engage Joe Public *– the agency tasked with promoting 'Make it Kenya' – an international brand campaign for the country showcasing tourism, commerce and investment opportunities to the world. The launch in September 2015 saw the unveiling of* MakeItKenya.com, *a digital portal for tourists, investors and the global media, aimed at providing rich and shareable content worldwide.*

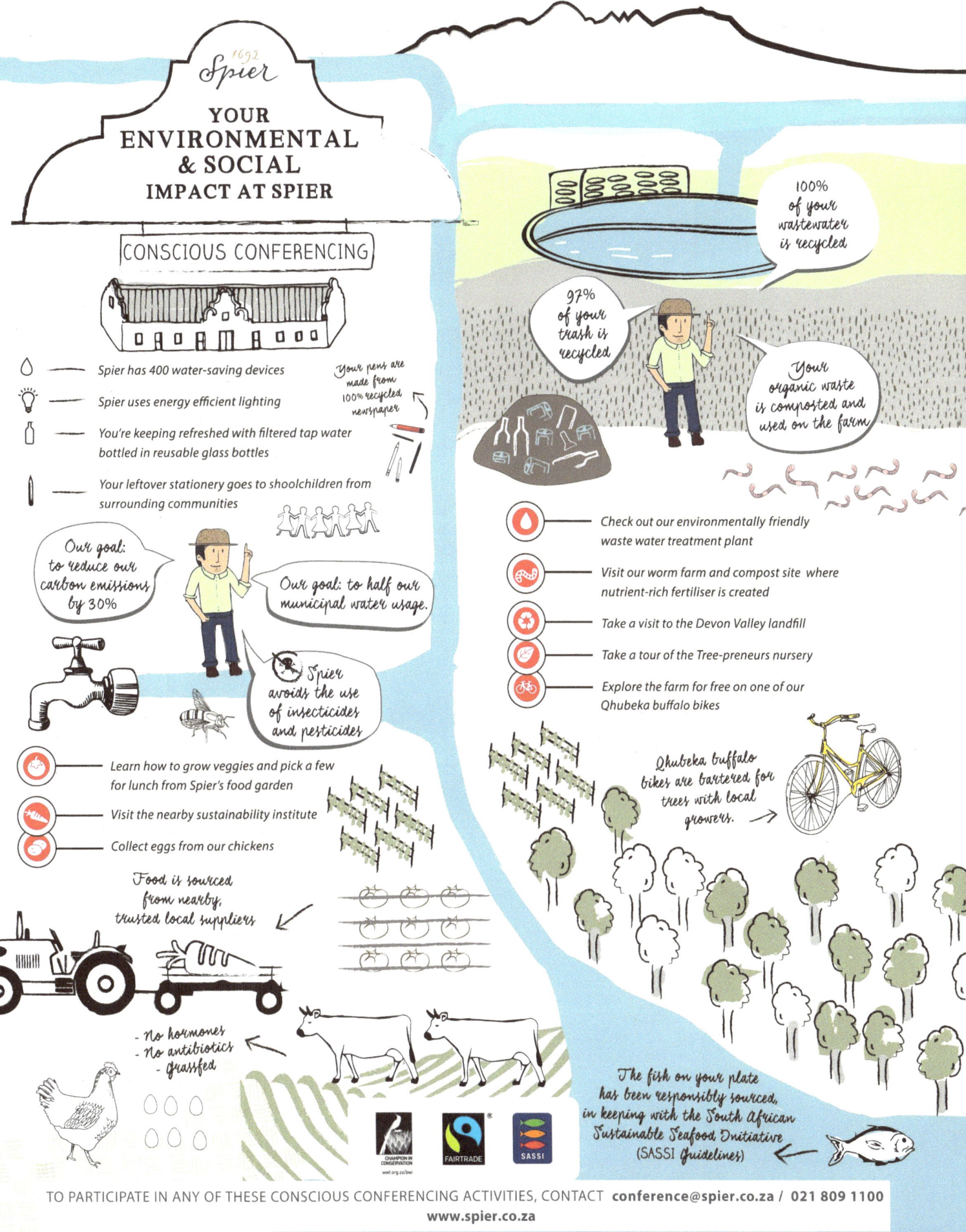

HOSPITALITY

Part-time Online Hotel Qualifications

Many leaners are not able to study full time for a hotel qualification as the need to earn an income comes first. The current volatile situation at universities further makes e-learning an attractive option, writes Christa Badenhorst.

Guvon Academy now offers a formal, accredited hotel qualification part-time – be that during your coffee breaks, lunch hour of after work. All that the student needs is Wi-Fi or an internet connection and an email address.

With the unemployment rate at 26.4% end of 2015 according to Fin24, 5.5 million SA citizens unemployed and a further 14.8 million people who are not economically active, we all know that to better yourself and your income potential, it makes sense to get a formal qualification and work experience behind your name.

Guvon Academy, based in Muldersdrift at Glenburn Lodge & Spa, added E-learning to its offering this year. The courses in Tourism, Events and Hospitality range from Kids Party planning, domestic worker courses to Executive Waiter and Barman, Events Management and Professional Chef qualifications, to mention a few.

Application is a simple process – new students can register online at www.guvonacademy.co.za by completing a form and returning it to the Academy. Unlike universities and colleges, E-students can enrol any time of the year. Upon paying a 50% deposit for the course, the student receives a log-in code and the course contents is immediately available online. Students can download the contents or choose to access the material on the internet. To ease the financial strain, a monthly payment plan is available.

Courses are competitively priced and range from R450 per module (one month) up to the professional cookery qualification which is for 12 months at R15 000pp. Students are tested on completed modules with an online quiz. Live chats and live skype demonstrations are available to assist leaners. Some courses require a practical training component which will be done at one of the six Guvon Hotel properties.

Upon completion of the course, students may be absorbed in the hotel group should vacancies be available and the student qualifies for the position.

For more info on available courses, see www.guvonacademy.co.za. Contact Sonia Peel on +27 (0)11 668 1621/28 or (0)79 772 6886 or email sonia@guvonacademy.co.za

About the Author: Christa Badenhorst is the Group Marketing and PR manager at Guvon Hotels & Spas – a leading hospitality group offering a collection of hotels in Gauteng, Northwest and Mpumalanga.
All properties offer excellent accommodation, conference, team building and wedding facilities.
Kloofzicht Lodge & Spa, Glenburn Lodge & Spa and Bush Willow Tented Camp are in Muldersdrift, in the Cradle of Humankind.
Askari Game Lodge & Spa, a Big 5 game reserve, is in Magaliesberg, while Umbhaba Lodge is situated in Hazyview.
The Fairway Hotel, Spa & Golf Resort (Randpark Golf Club), and All Suite On 14th (Fairlands) add city retreats to the country collection of properties.

www.guvonhotels.co.za | Central Reservations +27 (0)8611 48866

Central Drakensberg

Set out on an adventure in the Champagne Valley...

For 57 years Gooderson Leisure has been making holiday experiences a memorable occasion, providing better value to keep families coming back for more.

Now Gooderson Leisure has brought more GOOD FUN to the Central Drakensberg's Champagne Valley!

With 36 NEW superior air-conditioned hotel rooms and 8 self-catering units **Gooderson Monks Cowl Golf Resort** is the ideal family resort from which to explore the Champagne Valley.

The improved 9-hole, 18 Tee NGU rated golf course; NEW 18 hole Adventure Golf Course, large NEW rock swimming pool with slides and NEW Spa plus a host of activities in near proximity will ensure a fun-filled getaway and great value.

Gooderson Monks Cowl
Golf Resort

Reservations: +27 (0)36 468 1300 | Email: monksadmin@goodersons.co.za | www.goodersonleisure.co.za
Gooderson Leisure Est. 1957

MARKETING

TripAdvisor at 16, The Facts

TripAdvisor is no stranger to the travel trade but did you know that it started life above a tiny pizza parlour called Kostas in the town of Needham, Massachusetts, USA in February 2000, writes **Peter Corcoran**.

Sixteen years later and TripAdvisor has grown to become the largest and most popular travel website in the world. It has a highly engaged community posting comments, answering questions, uploading images and giving feedback to hoteliers, restaurateurs and hospitality industry operators.

However, it is not just a single website but in fact the TripAdvisor group owns 23 other travel websites. These include AirfareWatchdog, Jetsetter and Virtual Tourist. TripAdvisor branded websites get in excess of 350 million unique visitors per month combined and the company now operates in 47 countries worldwide in 28 languages.

The real success of the brand has been its user-generated-content business model and how wildly successful this has been. For example, 2,600 new topics are posted by users across the TripAdvisor forums daily and more than four out of five questions that are posed in the English-speaking forums get answered within hours!

The user-generated-content model has also enabled users to upload more than 46 million images snapped by themselves to the site. For a visual illustration of the power of TripAdvisor today in 2016 and a look at where it began, view this infographic created by SunSearch Holidays.

View the full infographic on the Tourism Tattler website.

TripAdvisor is the world's largest travel website & community.
It allows travellers to plan, book & review their perfect trip.
Millions of travellers around the world look to it for user generated content & advice.

TripAdvisor will celebrate 16 years in business this February 2016.

10 Facts You May Not Know About TripAdvisor

1. It was founded above a pizza shop named Kostas in Needham, Massachusetts.
2. The 1st ever review was of Captain's House Inn in Chatham, Massachusetts.
3. In the TripAdvisor owl logo, the 2 eye colours represent the way travellers choose where to go (green) & where not to go (red).
4. The average rating is positive at more than 4 out of 5.*
5. The most reviewed city is London with 1.8 million+ reviews.*
6. There are more restaurants listed than hotels.
7. The most reviewed country is the USA.
8. The least reviewed country is Tuvalu.
9. The majority of its traffic comes from outside the USA.
10. The total word count of all reviews is 10 billion+.*

*Note: Statistics as of February 2015.

TripAdvisor By the Numbers

Operations

- 47 Countries worldwide.
- 23 Other travel media brands & websites that it manages & operates.
- 3,000+ Employees.
- 28 Languages.
- 350 Million+ Unique monthly visitors on TripAdvisor branded websites.
- 90 Million+ Marketable members worldwide.

About the author: Peter Corcoran is the Owner and Director of SunSearch Holidays, based in Dublin, Ireland. www.sunsearchholidays.ie

Legal

FROM THE BENCH™
With Louis the Lawyer
BENCHMARK ©

CPA: The Consumer Protection Act

- Part 2 -
CANCELLATION, PENALTIES & NON-REFUNDABLE DEPOSITS

NOTE: The Risk in Tourism series (The Law: Contracts) will continue with Part 18 in a future edition.

SECTION 16: DIRECT MARKETING AND COOLING OFF

This section entitles the consumer to cancel a transaction 'resulting from' direct marketing i.e. [Section 16 (3)]

A consumer may rescind a transaction resulting from any direct marketing without reason or penalty, by notice to the supplier in writing, or another recorded manner and form, within five business days after the later of the date on which—

(a) the transaction or agreement was concluded; or

(b) the goods that were the subject of the transaction were delivered to the consumer.

The supplier must return to the consumer any payment received which reimbursement must be within 15 business days from the date of the notice or return of the goods [Section 16 (4)(a)].

Notwithstanding the wording of section 16 (3) i.e. 'without reason or penalty', the supplier not without remedy/right of recourse i.e. the supplier may rely on section 20 (6) [Section 16 (4)(b)] i.e. the supplier may charge the consumer as follows: 'a reasonable amount for use of the goods during the time they were in the consumer's possession'.

SECTION 17: CONSUMER'S RIGHT TO CANCEL RESERVATION, ADVANCE BOOKING

This section of the Consumer Protection Act (CPA) is often seen as the sole issue to be considered – as you can see from my article, nothing can be further from the truth!

The first aspect to bear in mind is that the consumer is entitled to cancel [Section 17 (2)].

The supplier IS entitled to (a) require 'reasonable deposit in advance' (b) 'impose a reasonable charge for cancellation' [Section 17 (3)].

Such a charge will be 'unreasonable if it exceeds a fair amount in the circumstances' – what the latter is, is not clear but the following factors need to be considered may well comprise such 'circumstances':
- Nature of the goods or services
- Length of cancellation notice given by consumer
- The 'reasonable potential' of the supplier finding an alternative consumer
- 'The general practice of the relevant industry'.

The above penalty may not be imposed if 'the person for whom, or for whose benefit the booking, reservation or order was made' dies or is hospitalized – note it is only the actual pax who gets this benefit.

SECTION 33: CATALOGUE MARKETING

Described as a transaction entered into in person and includes an agreement by telephone 'postal order or fax, or in any similar manner' – one would imagine that the latter can/does include online transactions.

The supplier must disclose its 'cancellation, return, exchange and refund policies' [Section 33 (3)(f)].

Bear in mind that such disclosure must meet all the (other) requirements e.g. plain language, conspicuous etc.

SECTION 41: FALSE, MISLEADING OR DECEPTIVE REPRESENTATIONS

This section applies to 'marketing' but bear in mind it has not been defined as such – however 'market' has been defined as being the promotion and supply of goods and we've seen how widely these phrases are defined!

The part of this section that applies to our topic is the duty on the supplier not only to ensure that the wording used is not misleading, ambiguous or deceptive but to clarify 'any apparent misapprehension' that the client may have.

Such a 'misapprehension' may be reasonably apparent from the client's body language e.g. frowning if it is a one-on-one sale but very difficult when it is telephonic or on-line. Accordingly the documentation and on-line information must be carefully scrutinized to ensure that such 'misapprehension' is avoided and addressed.

This section [Section 41 (3)] has a so-called deeming provision i.e. if the following misapprehension is not corrected, it will be deemed/regarded to be a 'false, misleading or deceptive presentation' and I believe this includes not very clearly explaining non-refundable deposit and cancellation provisions i.e.

(i) the transaction affects, or does not affect, any rights, remedies or obligations of a consumer.

To be continued in the April edition.

Disclaimer:
This article is intended to provide a brief overview of legal matters pertaining to the travel and tourism industry and is not intended as legal advice.
© Adv Louis Nel, 'Louis The Lawyer', March 2016.

RISK

Understanding Tourism Trade Insurance
- Part 3 -

Part 1 in this series covered an introduction to insurance, an outline on the EC Directive, the basics of risk management, and financial guarantees. Part 2 looked at liability insurance, and Part 3 concludes his subject, writes **Des Langkilde**.

TYPES OF INSURANCE
The five kinds of insurance that apply to the tourism industry:
1. Financial Guarantee (Insurance Bond) - *Refer January issue*.
2. Liability Insurance
3. Vehicle / Property Insurance
4. Travel Insurance / Medical Rescue
5. Other Business Insurance (Buy & Sell, Key Person, Provident Fund)

How much Passenger Liability cover do you need?

As a general rule of thumb, the cover you need depends on the average number of passengers that you transport at any one time and the net worth of the individuals that you are transporting. Some policies recommend one million per seat but this does not make sense as it is more likely that one passenger in an accident will be more seriously injured than others and one million will not be enough to cover that one person in the event of serious injury.

> **TIP:** It is better to ensure that the indemnity limit covers all occupants of a particular vehicle, on a per incident, per occurrence basis, regardless of the number of passengers.

Of course, the number of passengers that your vehicle is licensed to carry does make a difference in calculating the cover amount required. For instance, ten million may be sufficient for a microbus but a coach may need as much as 100 million cover.

Let's look at the sequence of events that could occur in the event of a serious bus or minibus accident:

- The accident occurs, quite often in a remote area in bad conditions and with limited communication facilities. If the driver or guide is able, they will immediately seek medical assistance, either by phone or by alerting passing motorists. This might be done by a passer-by, a nearby landowner or even by a surviving passenger. Obviously the first priority is to tend to anyone in need of immediate medical attention, and those in desperate need may require airlifting. Normally the police are alerted at this stage and they will take eyewitness reports as well as a statement from the driver if he is able. No one can control the exact chain of events in accidents and one can only hope that common sense prevails and guardian angels are close at hand.
- At some stage the head office of the company involved will be alerted to the disaster. These are the calls that we all live in fear of receiving. They are very difficult to handle if made by a hysterical client or any third party and one must ensure that every attempt is made to only deal with a responsible logical person who can speak English and who understands the ways of the country where the accident has occurred. Obviously the ideal person is a member of your staff wherever possible. At this stage a senior member of the company involved must take responsibility for coordinating the whole event and this person must be mentally and procedurally equipped for the task at hand. This will often entail dealing with medical rescue teams and liaising with nearby accommodation establishments.
- An accurate factual report must be drawn up as soon as possible, preferably with input from your driver. This must not try and apportion blame but it must be to the point, with all relevant facts that any next of kin would need to know. Along with this one must try and ascertain the status of each and every client and their whereabouts relating to their injuries and to which hospital or doctor they have been transferred. Once in possession of this, this report should be made available to overseas agents for their information and for the next of kin. This report must not accept any liability but it must be factually accurate, as obviously one must not cause undue distress to anxious relatives. Such a report may be made available to the press should they already have been alerted.
- Your local insurance company or broker must also be informed as to what has happened so that they can also start to get their procedures under way. This is important, as it is ultimately the insurance assessor who will play a vital role in deciding the extent of liability if any and he can also act as the go-between your clients and your company.
- It is ideal to get a senior member of staff to the site of the accident as soon as possible. This is a difficult task as this individual is likely to take abuse and to bear the brunt of all sorts of accusations. As people are injured and traumatised they feel vulnerable and expect your company to take care of everything and pay for absolutely all incurred costs. It is a very difficult tightrope that the responsible person must walk, and there are no hard and fast rules here. Obviously where possible your company must assist all passengers in getting to a place of comfort or to medical attention. It is at this stage that one has to ascertain the insurance that each passenger is carrying and attempt to alert these companies abroad. Unfortunately many clients still do not carry sufficient travel insurance, and some none at all. It is for these eventualities

that all companies in Southern Africa should INSIST THAT ALL PAX TRAVELLING ON THEIR TOURS HAVE COMPULSORY COVER and details of such cover must be recorded at the start of the tour and kept on record in case of an emergency. In the heat of the moment it is very difficult to decide to what financial extent one is obliged to go. Distraught passengers will request five star accommodation, phone calls all over the world, first class flights back home and the like. Should you oblige these requests and run up huge accounts on their behalf, you are unlikely to ever recover these. These expenses are what their insurance should be picking up and should not be for your company's account.

- Your own insurance company should agree to cover a limited amount of comfort expenses, which could obviously alleviate an unpleasant situation but try and get clearance for this from the assessor or better still, check that it exists in the policy wording prior to obtaining cover. It sounds terrible to have to think of money whilst people are in pain and bleeding but this is the reality of the world in which we live. Remember that accidents will happen, whether your company is at fault or not and EVERYONE must carry insurance for this eventuality.
- A necessary task here is also that of offering any uninjured or unaffected passengers the opportunity of carrying on the tour in another vehicle, with another guide, should they so desire. Obviously this will depend on numerous factors and generally it is unlikely that anyone will wish to continue in the event of a serious accident. However some clients may well wish to still try and make the most out of their remaining stay and your company is obliged to try and comply with this request if possible.
- Once clients are all in good medical hands or at a place of comfort with access to communication links, the role of the mediator is over. Clients have to take control of their own individual situation and agents have to alert next of kin and activate things from their side. Monies paid out of pocket by your company justifiably may be claimed from your insurance company. Only after the assessor has completed this task will liability be apportioned. This is actually an issue for the insurance companies and does not really affect you. Should your company be liable for whatever reason, and you are sufficiently covered, your insurer will handle all claims and they should be settled. In most cases negligence is very hard to prove and the onus will be on the individual client to be sufficiently covered.
- In the event of a death of a client in an accident, the body will eventually be sent to a local mortuary. The process of repatriating the body to its country of origin is complicated and bureaucratic. The costs associated with this would normally be covered under your client's personal funeral policy or travel insurance policy, which again highlights the need to record such details prior to undertaking a tour.
- Finally when all the dust has settled, a reality that your company must face is the recovery of the vehicle. This can be costly and is only covered under the vehicle's comprehensive insurance policy.

Obviously such an accident is every company's worst nightmare but one must be prepared for it because the manner in which you handle it can mean the difference between the success or failure of your company.

Below is a list of pointers that an efficient operator must have in place to avoid unnecessary risk and the risk of being liable:

- In South Africa, the driver / guide must be legal in all respects. He must carry the correct driver's licence, a valid Professional Drivers Permit (PrDP) and if applicable a valid tourist guides licence;
- The driver must have had adequate rest prior to the accident so that fatigue cannot be cited as a factor contributing to the cause of the crash;
- Obviously the driver must not be under the influence of alcohol or any drugs at the time of the accident. Should he or she have consumed an unreasonable amount of alcohol or be perceived to have partied until late the night before, this could count against you;
- The vehicle must have been mechanically sound prior to the accident. A proven service record will help. Tyre wear will always be a critical factor;
- The speed at the time of the accident will be crucial;
- A company's past accident free record will certainly be in your favour;
- Should the driver have undertaken any driving training, this would be of tremendous help;
- Eyewitness accounts must be followed up, road surface and visibility conditions must be noted;
- Extra precautions like safety belts throughout the vehicle will also count in your favour.

Sometimes no matter what precautions you take, an accident will still occur. The human factor will always play a role, hence the need for insurance. Unavoidable negligence is not a crime. Even if your company is found liable, it does not mean that you will not be covered. In fact quite the opposite - that is the very reason why you are insured. Obviously the extent of the negligence is a factor, as is the extent of injury to a client. It is for these reasons that this cover has to be substantial. One can imagine the claim when an individual is paralysed for life and you are at fault. Where a company can be crippled is when they are guilty of blatant negligence and their cover is either non-existent or inadequate.

*This article, to be continued in the April 2016 edition of the Tourism Tattler, will explain the **Road Accident Fund Amendment Bill** and the impact that this Act has had on Passenger Liability insurance in South Africa and on foreign tourists in particular - **Ed**.*

TRANSPORT

Overland Tour Vehicle Of Choice

The "relevant technology for purpose" principle employed by Hino in designing, engineering and building its range of 500-Series trucks has found favour with Drifters, a division of Tourvest Holdings.

What this means is that these Hino 1626 truck chassis-cabs, which form the basis of a fleet of 18 overland safari vehicles, are proving very Africa-friendly in terms of reliability, durability, ease of maintenance and repair when operating in remote regions in Africa.

"We are very satisfied with the performance of the Hinos in operations that are varied but can be very tough, particularly when storms ruin the gravel roads and rivers rise," said Steve Maidment, Operations Director at Drifters. "Our overland vehicles, which each carry 16 tourists, are often more than 1 000 kilometres from the nearest dealer, so reliability is very important."

Maidment went on to say that the Hino truck-based safari vehicles have now clocked up 3.6-million kilometres, often under harsh conditions and have been virtually trouble free except for a couple of broken spring blades and a differential spider gear breaking due to getting stuck and spinning the rear wheel.

"The reason is that these trucks are built strong, with big wheel bearings and drive shafts. Importantly many of the steering, suspension and transmission parts have grease nipples, adding to the ease of maintenance and subsequent reliability. They certainly make my life easier!"

Drifters, which was established in 1983 with one well-used minibus, has grown significantly over the years and now has 30 full-time guides. A variety of different brands and vehicle types have been used for its touring operations in Africa.

The switch to Hino came in 2010 after a lengthy study and evaluation of potentially suitable vehicles available on the local market. There are now 18 of these Hino vehicles being used in operations that extend from five to 24 days, with the latter trip involving travelling from Cape Town to Johannesburg via Namibia, Botswana, Zambia and Zimbabwe. Other countries which are on the Drifters extensive schedule are Mozambique, Kenya, Uganda, Malawi, Kenya and Tanzania.

Drifters now operates a fleet of 18 Hino 500-Series 1626 chassis cabs converted into 16-seater overland safari vehicles.

Steve Maidment, Operations Director at Drifters, displaying the novel fold-out kitchen incorporated into the innovative bodies developed and built by Drifters at the company's facility near Muldersdrif.

These tours operate on tight schedules and most of the tourists are from overseas, especially Germans, Netherlanders, Belgians and Scandinavians so the reliability of the transport is vital in terms of meeting the timetable and providing outstanding customer service. The success of the Drifters business can be seen in the many tourists who return to South Africa to participate in other Drifters tours after their first experience.

A very important factor in the Drifters operation is that all the safari vehicle bodies are tailor-made by the company itself. These vehicles are unique in that they have to transport a full complement of camping equipment, such as tents, stretchers and chairs, as well as being equipped with a refrigerator, freezer, food storage area and a self-contained kitchen unit with cooking and washing up facilities.

The manufacturing facility is based in Muldersdrift, near Krugersdorp. A number of bus and truck body builders were used in the early days to build safari vehicles, but the requirements are so specialised that it was decided to take manufacture of the vehicle bodies in house. This was a bold move that has proved very successful over many years.

This facility where the vehicles are built also houses the maintenance and repair workshop as well as the various storerooms and a facility for making and repairing the tents. It has a staff complement of 15 people.

The frames of the safari vehicle body and several of the panels are made of stainless steel, which is corrosion resistant, while most body panels are made of glassfibre, which is light, strong and easy to repair when necessary. Some of the bodies are 8-9 years old and showing no sign of corrosion. The vehicles themselves cover between 70 000 - 80 000 kilometres a year. They are serviced at Hino Honeydew while under warranty and then maintained by Drifters at the Muldersdrift workshop.

Very few outside suppliers are used in the construction of the safari vehicles; even the electrical wiring and trimming is carried out in-house. Each vehicle has dual fuel tanks, each with a capacity of 450 litres and special features on the filler system to deter fuel theft. There is a 400-litre water tank. Huge, panoramic windows which can be opened provide an excellent view of the scenery for the occupants, who are seated on adjustable Isringhausen seats as used in many truck cabs.

The design and construction methods for conceptualising and building these unique vehicles have been fine-tuned over the years and the latest models are ideal for this type of nomadic operation, often in remote areas of the continent. The bodies can be removed from one truck chassis and bolted onto another one, which a big plus.

Drifters manages its own tyres which often involves repairing punctures and other damage or scrapping tyres before the tread is worn down due to damage in off-road operations. The large wheels, with 10 studs, and the large tyres are other features of the Hino which make them well-suited to this overland touring operation.

The man behind the designing and building of the safari vehicles as well as all the other aspects of this complex operation is Steve Maidment, who joined the company as a tour guide in 1990. Over the ensuing years he has been instrumental in many of the innovations and initiatives which keep Drifters at the top of its game.

For more information visit www.drifters.co.za and www.hino.co.za

www.ingramcontent.com/pod-product-compliance
Lightning Source LLC
Chambersburg PA
CBHW050431180526
45159CB00005B/2491